# EXPLORING CLAY
## Hand Techniques

Rolf Hartung
# Exploring Clay
Hand Techniques

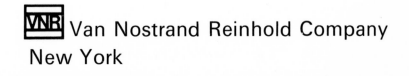 Van Nostrand Reinhold Company
New York

Van Nostrand Reinhold Company Regional Offices:
New York Cincinnati Chicago Millbrae Dallas

German edition copyright © 1971 by Otto Maier Verlag, Ravensburg,
Germany

English translation copyright © 1972 by Litton Educational Publishing,
Inc.

Library of Congress Catalog Card Number: 79-178699
ISBN 0 442 23176 8

Published in the United States of America by
Van Nostrand Reinhold Company
450 West 33rd Street, New York, N.Y. 10001

# Contents

# Introduction

To be satisfying, utensils such as dishes, pots, cups, and mugs need a harmony of shape and function.

The interior of a vessel is of special importance if it is to be used for food to be kept, prepared, divided, or consumed. On the other hand, the external shape must meet the requirements of grasping, encircling, and carrying by hands.

In working with clay in hollow shapes these requirements are best fulfilled if hands, our most basic tool, are used for kneading, drawing, pressing, and compressing.

For example, when we broaden out a kneaded clay ball to form a hollow body, we obtain earthenware that grows from within, with its exterior shaped out of the grip and movements of the hands. Content and form become 'graspable'. Inside and outside are in harmony.

Over and above the recognition of the basic functions, clay also allows experimentation to discover optimum practical forms, as in the joining of clay parts in large vessels.

In order to let the hands do most of the work, only a few tools have been introduced in this book, even for finishing.

Rolf Hartung

# Clay

## Origin and occurrence

From prehistoric times clay has been essential to man. Its origin is traced to aluminous minerals freed by the weathering of stone. Carried along for some distance by the water, the clayey constituents sink to the bottom when they reach standing water. In the waterway they mix with organic remains, metal oxides, sand, etc. After thousands of years clay strata are formed out of these drift-deposits. Such deposits occur all over the world. Clays, often covered with only a shallow layer of soil, can be collected in delta formations of lakes and pools, damp hollows, and erosion areas.

## Collecting and preparing

The large lumps of clay dug out of the deposits are broken up, placed in walled basins and covered with water. Heavy impurities sink to the bottom in the mud. The water above is run off and the clay mud is put through a sieve.
The clay is then poured on plaster trays and when it begins to dry it is kneaded until it is homogeneous, that is until it has the same density throughout. To this end portions are divided and re-divided, clapped together and kneaded. This is a strenuous process. For this reason, today, clay is almost always prepared by machine. It can be obtained ready for use from potters or speciality dealers, in rolls of about 6 in. diameter and 20–30 lb. weight.

## Water content

Clay and water are bound together in a twofold manner. All clay, even when in powder form, contains water in chemical and physical combination. According to the variety of clay the quantity of physically-combined water determines the plasticity, the workability.

## Storing

The mass of clay is stored in a box lined with sheet zinc or in plastic buckets with air-tight lids. In order to regulate the moistness we cover the clay with damp cloths.

## Drying of clay

Clay cannot be worked in large solid blocks as it will dry without cracking only to $1\frac{1}{2}$ in. wall-depth. In order to obtain wares of greater size than the drying depth permits, the larger forms should be produced as hollow bodies.

Clay walls dry from the outside inwards. Walls that are as even and strong as possible, a lump of clay that has been well and thoroughly kneaded beforehand, and a medium room-temperature, as well as protection from draughts and heat, are required conditions for drying out without tensions. Individual projecting parts such as handles and spouts should be protected by damp cloths to prevent them from drying out too quickly. The moisture should evaporate evenly from all sides. It is therefore advisable to place the ware on a rack and turn it repeatedly.

## Drying out stages

We distinguish between three stages of hardness:
1 Moist-hard, still workable for a few hours.
2 Leather-hard, after about a day, suitable for cutting, beating, and attaching parts.
3 Hard, may still be worked with abrasive paper and can be fired after about a week.

Size, wall-thickness, and temperature dictate time differences in the drying process. Dried clay works are hard but not resilient. They break easily. Dried clay may be kneaded again if softened in water.

## Shrinkage

As clay dries out the particles draw closer together. The volume of the earthenware diminishes. This shrinkage may be measured on scratches 4 in. long for instance. 1/25 in. then represents 1 per cent. To the shrinkage caused by air, later the shrinkage caused by firing must be added. (In all 8–10 per cent.)

## Differences in clay

These already exist from the proportions of silica and alum earth. To these must be added oxides such as iron oxide, which colours the clay red in firing, or manganese oxide as a black colourant. Minerals that are admixed alter the plasticity. Clay is generally divided into three groups:

### 1 Fat clay

Fat clay gets its name from its smooth surface and its oily shine. Many extremely fine mud particles lie one beside the other. The gaps between them hold considerable amounts of water. The density of the material, however, makes it difficult for the water to penetrate the clay and to evaporate slowly from the inside. As fat clay dries appreciably more rapidly on the surface than inside, the differing inner and outer shrinkage causes splitting of the drying clay surface.
Its plasticity in a moist state, on the other hand, makes it suitable for sculptural sketching.

### 2 Thin clay

In contrast to fat clay, thin clay has an uneven, rough consistency. Its surface is matt. The fine mud particles are sometimes mixed with very coarse sand.
The consistency is therefore relatively loose. Because of the larger solid parts, less water is taken in than by fat clay. The loose structure allows the clay walls to dry out quickly and evenly. Since it is not easy to knead, and proves brittle in smaller work, it is used for clay plates or large built-up vessels. In this case the rapid drying permits the lower levels to bear the structure of the upper in a short time. Greek potters built vases up to 13 ft. high.

### 3 Medium clay

For our work we choose a clay of medium consistency. It should be easy to shape, to knead, and to draw. It must also be firm enough to take the heights that we determine by hand measure. It must be porous enough to dry pliantly without splitting.
Sometimes such favourable mixtures are to be found in clay beds. In general, however, the clays are mixed with additional substances. One then speaks of a mass mixing in which the clay is prepared for specific areas of use, for instance, for pressing, casting, throwing, or kneading. Suitable prepared clays may be purchased. For our purposes a medium clay that goes under the name of potter's clay is practical. If we wish to make this clay for ourselves we mix a fat clay with grog (ground potsherds) of $1/50 - 1/16$ in. granular texture or with quartz up to 25 per cent of the weight (when dealing with dry clay). Here one can experiment according to the explicit purposes.

## Firing

Small pieces of plaster and lime are *hydrophile*, i.e., extremely water-absorbent. When heated they split the article being fired. Air bubbles also expand and tear the clay walls. Such inadvertent enclosures must therefore be guarded against.

Clay that has dried hard and been fired is transformed in the heat of the kiln; the clay becomes pot. It is no longer soluble in water. Organic admixtures, which have partly determined the colour of the clay, are burnt. There are white-, red-, yellow- and black-firing natural clays.

Instead of the earlier wood-heated kilns we now have electric ones in which the temperature can be regulated. The heat-regulation facilitates the supervision of the firing process.

Two processes may be distinguished:
a)  biscuit firing and
b)  sharp or glost firing.

In biscuit firing we stack the articles to be fired. They may be placed closely against and on top of one another, touching one another.

Closing the kiln door and turning on the heat are always events. It will now be revealed whether we were careful and whether we are in luck. We are full of joy and doubt.

The kiln flue is opened. The first stage eliminates the mechanically-bound water from the clay. During a period of two to three hours the temperature should be brought up to 570°F. (300°C.). The water will exude from the pores in the clay, but too rapid heating will prevent the water from being sweated out. Instead, it will expand and spoil the articles being fired. Slow heating ensures precision in the first stage, the success of the firing. In the second stage, up to about 1100°F. (600°C.), we close the flue, after a glass held to the outlet shows no further steam (depending on the earthenware and the firing time, at 570°–750°F. (300°– 400°C.).

In the third stage, 1100°–1650°F. (600°– 900°C.), the chemically-bound water has evaporated. At 1650°F. (900°C.) the biscuit firing is finished. The clay has become pot. In all, the process lasts about eight to nine hours.

Cooling must follow slowly. The kiln door should be opened a little at 212°F. (100°C.) at the earliest. Even then it is safer to wait. Curiosity has caused many a break.

In sharp firing the pot is heated up to 2000°F. (1100°C.). The fired pot vitrifies between 1800°F. (1000°C.) and 2000°F. (1100°C.). The impurities in the clay become liquid and close the pores. This produces watertight earthenware (stoneware), often with a deep reddish-brown hue. Above the vitrifying-point is the melting-point. The pure clay does not melt, but the impurities do. The ware being fired collapses.

10

## Colour applications

1 Engobes

Engobes are finely-ground natural coloured clays. They are mixed with water and put through a narrow-meshed sieve. The colours thus naturally obtained, white, yellow, brick-red, and black, since they may also be mixed with one another, give a wide range of tints that discreetly harmonize with the plastic forms of the earthenware. In addition, the surface can be kept as colourful as desired with different oxides. It should be borne in mind, however, that gaudy colour disturbs the form.

For engobing, the earthenware must be leather-hard. The dry engobe then adapts itself to the drying-shrinkage of the vessel. Dipping and spraying are methods that may be adopted. Where the inner and outer walls are engobed, the second engobing should take place after the first application has dried.

A rubber ball with a small tube replaces the painting horn formerly used to put in dots and lines. Moist-hard clay can be painted with a brush or stamped with foam-rubber shapes. Designs may be scratched into engobed surfaces. All decoration should, of course, serve the plastic form and not become an aim in itself.

2 Glazes

Glazing powder consists of a vitrifiable mixture of lead oxide, silicic acid, and additives. Having already been melted once and ground, it has acquired a favourable melting point.

These fused (baked) glazes are supplied in powder form. We stir them with water to a milky paste and press them through a very finely meshed sieve. Since the glaze constituents continually sink to the bottom, the liquid must be stirred frequently. The usual methods are rinsing out in the case of inside glazing, dipping and spraying in the case of outside glazing. A spray-gun can also be used.

The porous pot absorbs the water and the powdery glaze-dust sticks in the pores. Any excess, particularly on the bottom, is removed with a moist sponge. In the kiln, glazed articles must not touch one another. They are placed on tripods and triangular stands, otherwise the glaze running off them will glue the work fast to the surface it is standing on.

Engobed ware is given a transparent glaze.

Colour glazes require different temperatures when their melting points are not the same. Only temperature-co-ordinated glazes may be fired in one firing process.

The items that went in covered with powdery dust are taken out of the kiln transformed after successful firing to treasures in their glass-like or matt glowing finish.

1

From a well prepared lump of clay (1) we take a handful and knead a ball (2). Its diameter, depending on the size of one's hand, will be about $2\frac{1}{2}$–3 in. Clay can dry without splitting to a depth of $1\frac{1}{2}$ in. so that a solid clay ball should only have a diameter of 3 in. at the most.

The pressed and rolled clay must not stick to the hands and must not be brittle when moulded into shapes. As the warmth of the hands and also the room temperature always draw out a certain amount of moisture, we should work without interruption. Between work periods we can prevent undesirable drying-out by wrapping the clay in moist cloth or a piece of plastic.

2

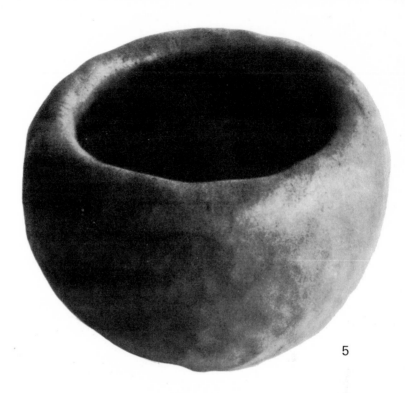

5

For ware within the scope of hand-shaping (6–8 in.), drawing the clay is recommended as an elementary work process. To get the feel of it, to make it develop out of the hand, one should practise for a long time just shaping a clay ball. For the hollow shape subsequently formed from the ball, three basic directions apply:

a) **Breaking up** the ball: the thumb of one hand is pressed into the ball of clay, while turning the ball against the inside of the other hand (3).

b) **Laying the bottom** of the hollow shape: the thickness of the bottom section is determined by the feel of it. The bottom surface is pressed, drawn, and smoothed from inside and outside.

c) **Drawing up** (4) and smoothing (5) the side walls.

6

7

8

The basic form (5) can be developed in different ways: the thumb of one hand draws clay spirally upwards. At the same time the index and middle fingers, slightly bent and lying one against the other, press against the thumb from the outside. The working of clay demands pressure and counter-pressure. While the drawing hand remains roughly on the same spot, the fingers of the other hand turn the clay shape in a counter-movement.

The position in which the hand holds the clay gives rise to three variations:

a) The bottom of the ball shapes itself in the hollowed hand and takes the form of a parabola (6).

b) The bottom shapes itself in the flattened hand like a bowl. In example (7) the circular shape was finally pressed into an oval. It now corresponds to the inside of the hand.

c) Held between the fingers, the bowl flares out conically (8).

9

10

11

The clay is pushed upwards as it is drawn.
Pressed tightly together, it dries without tension, without air bubbles, and therefore without any splits forming (9).
Walls of uneven height (10) are smoothed along their upper edges until they are of even height. At the edge of a vessel clay dries very quickly. Should splits occur through this, one can smooth them with a moistened finger.
Clay may also be compressed. Here it was pushed together between the thumb and index finger of both hands, coaxing the walls to curve gently inwards (11).
(Upper part: white engobe with transparent glaze. Lower part: black matt glaze.) In all three examples the base, developed out of the hollowed hand, is similar.

12

This vessel (12) has a projecting rim of a thumb's width, which facilitates pouring liquids. The pot can be lifted out of the fire with a gun rest. The three feet added increase its general usefulness.

In attaching functional parts such as feet, handles, spouts, etc., the joining points, which are still moist- to leather-hard, should be roughened with a piece of wood and painted with slip. Thus prepared, they bind when pressed together.

13

Clay feet

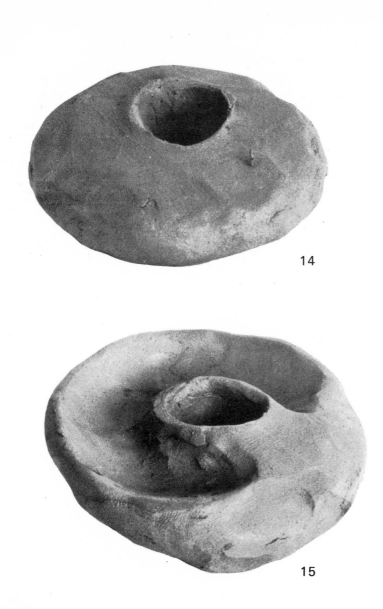

14

15

For this candleholder a flattened clay ball is pressed in this manner: the thumb of one hand forms the candle hold and at the same time acts as the turning axis for smoothing out the bowl shape with the thumb of the other hand. The part that remains untouched (15) becomes a handle when it is hollowed out underneath. However, the bowl may be completed (16) and the handle added afterwards (17).

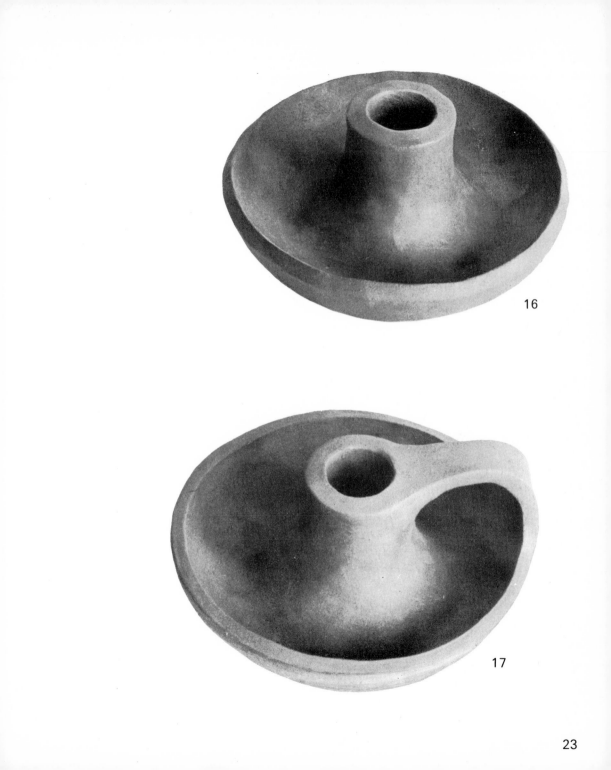

16

17

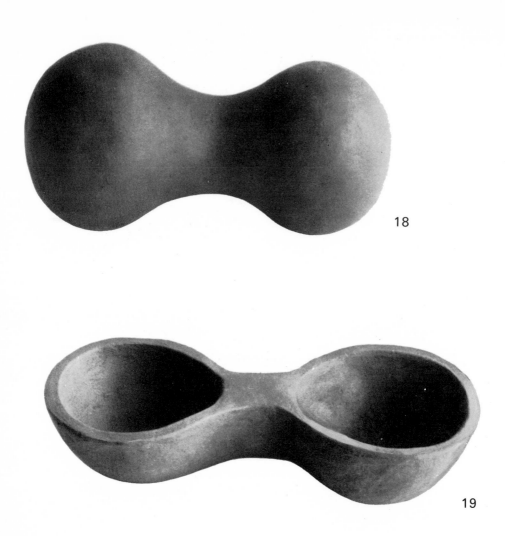

18

19

By squeezing with encircling thumb and index finger a round clay ball becomes a double ball (18). Then the double ball is cut in half with a wire cutter (a 1/32 in. thick, steel wire) and the hemispheres are hollowed out with fingers or a wire scoop (37) (if necessary, also use a spoon) and smoothed.

Pepper and salt (19).

20

Cups cut off the double ball (18) change it. We obtain a basic form in which the hollow hemi-spheres can be varied in size, width, depth, roundness, and distance from each other (20).

21

22

The base of the tambourine (21) is left solid at first, in order to support the kettle, and is later hollowed out. The eyelets hold the tension cords of the sounding skin.
For the elongated vase with eyelet loops, above, the lower hemisphere has been separated and developed into the circular base (22).

23

24

25

28

26

27

The bell (23) is also drawn out of the double ball. The handle is pierced through the centre to the sounding chamber to take the clapper, a clay ball tied on a thread (25).

Bell with black-and-white striped engobe and transparent glaze overcoating (26).

Bell with eyelet-handle, partly dipped in krater glaze (27).

Bells without clappers may also be incorporated in the carillon of clay bells. Harmonizing notes through size and shape requires experience.

28

29

In breaking up the hemisphere (28) the bottom is kept specially thick so that a ring for the drinking bowl (29) to stand on may be drawn out of the same mass. The bowl shows the form relation to figure 20.

30

30

31

The handle of the cup (30) is attached first by its thickened upper part. Then it is drawn between wet fingers into the desired shape and pressed on below.

Exterior parts that stand out from the main mass dry quickly and tear easily. Damp cloths will prevent them from drying out too fast.

On the bowl (31) the spout gives the vessel a one-sided profile.

32

By means of a mould (32) we can press vessels in a series. The mould takes the place of our hand which would otherwise be holding the clay mass. It provides the counter-pressure. Plaster moulds are especially suitable. As plaster is absorbent, it assists the drying of the clay. The thin-walled bowls (33) become firm in 20 to 30 minutes. Since the mass of clay pressed in shrinks, the vessels are automatically released and can be lifted out easily.

Mass reproductions can also be obtained by pouring liquified clay into the mould. After a time so much water is absorbed by the plaster that a clay lining is formed in the mould and the excess clay can be poured out.

An ashtray pressed from a cylindrical plaster mould (34).

A plaster mould is prepared as follows: stand four walls on a smooth base of stone, glass, etc. Seal the joins with clay or plaster. The insides of the walls are insulated with soapy water.

Pour plaster into water until small islands show above the surface. After stirring for a short time, pour the paste into the box-shaped form. After the plaster has stiffened, excess plaster is removed to give the mould the desired shape.

33

34

33

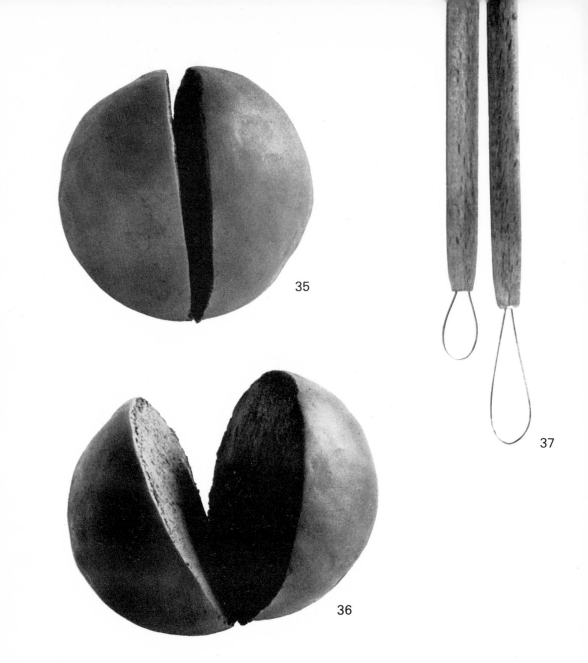

35

36

37

Halves of the clay ball that has been cut open (35, 36) can be hollowed out with a twined or smooth wire scoop (37), smoothed and put together again to form a hollow sphere (38).

38

39

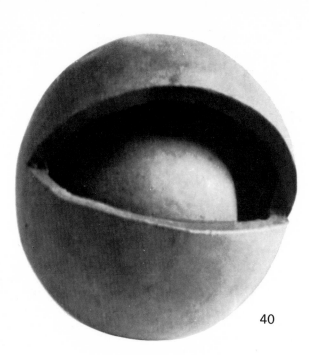

40

For firing, the clay balls must have an air-hole, otherwise the hot air will expand and burst the walls (40, 41, 42 and 43).

In biscuit firing the clay articles touch each other without fusing. This peculiarity enables us to enclose one ball in another (40).

If the inside ball is moist we can wrap it in paper before we put the second ball around it. To show the process, the sheath of the ball-rattle (40) was cut open when it was leather-hard.

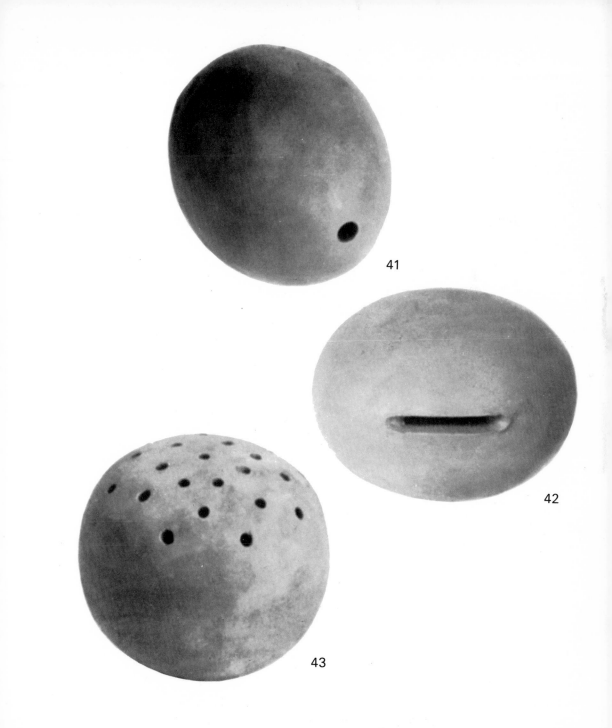

41

42

43

Clay chains can be made of hollow balls (44). Small solid balls are cut in half and pressed into a bowl shape with the thumb. When put together they may be biscuit fired, engobed and glazed. In the latter case we place the balls on heat-resistant, chrome-nickel wires, since tripods leave patches without glaze in the firing and also stick. Holes for threading, or other small apertures, are protected from dripping glaze by wooden sticks, which turn to charcoal during the firing.

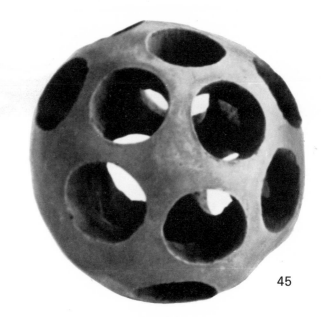

45

46

The durability of clay bridges may be observed in the structure of the hollow ball pierced with holes (45), which has remained intact. That a hollowed object may be as small as a kernel is shown by the hollow ball formed over the head of a pin (46).

47

The technique of cutting, hollowing out, and smoothing together gives even those with little experience the opportunity to prepare large hollow bodies.

The spherical pot (47) shows the addition of rolls of clay in rings as aids to grasping, and also for widening the lip at the spout.

48

In the case of the spherical pot with handle and spout (48) the function of pouring is primarily considered. The spout was obtained from a tube drawn from a rod. This and the attached handle are joined to the sphere to form a unit.

49

50

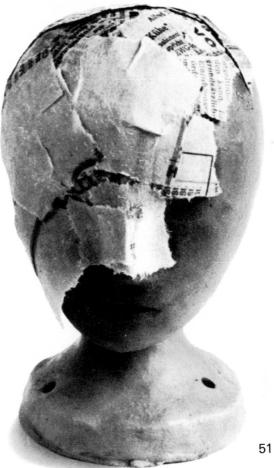

51

The clay model for dolls' heads in papier-mâché is obtained from the double ball hollowed out with a wire scoop (49, 50).

The fired hollow shape (51) is first covered with wet paper, and then a covering of paper pulp and paste is built up in layers.

The porous pot draws out moisture. After a time the papier-mâché can be cut apart and removed.

52

In drawing hemispheres one also wants, after some practice, to be able to build the clay walls higher. As clay lends itself not only to drawing and stretching but also to compressing and pressing together, the shaping of a spherical casing in one piece is possible (52).

53

The spherical bottle, which has been drawn with a neck (53), has a black krater glaze, applied by the dipping method. The glaze contrasts with the smooth, red-fired pot.

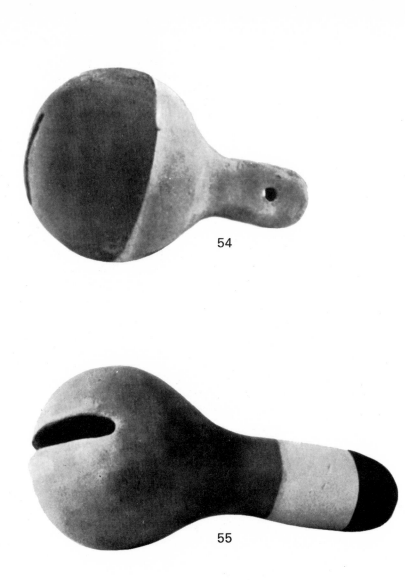

54

55

In the rattle (54) clay balls are enclosed as rattling stones. The flattened handle has been drawn out of the clay mass, not added. The other rattle (55), on the contrary, has a hollow-drawn handle.

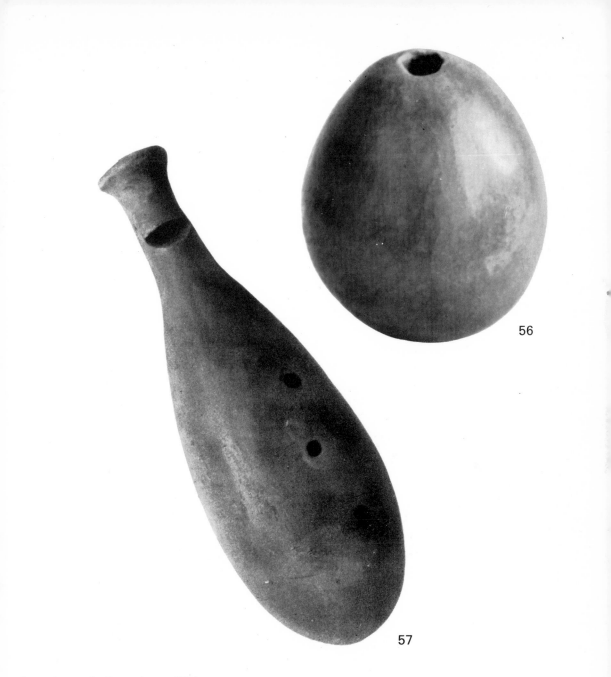

Oval drawn hollow shape (56).

The mouthpiece of the clay flute (57) is pierced through with a round rod. A slit for the lip divides the air-stream for the resonance box. It is cut into the leather-hard clay.

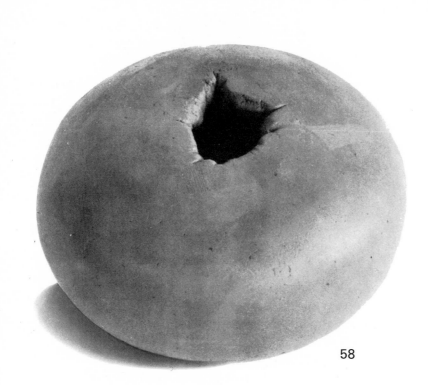

58

A sphere that has been flattened at its opposite ends (58) may be variously used as a starting point for bowls, pans, vases, bottles, and pots.

The tube for the neck of the vase (59) was attached after the top was dry enough to be capable of supporting it.

59

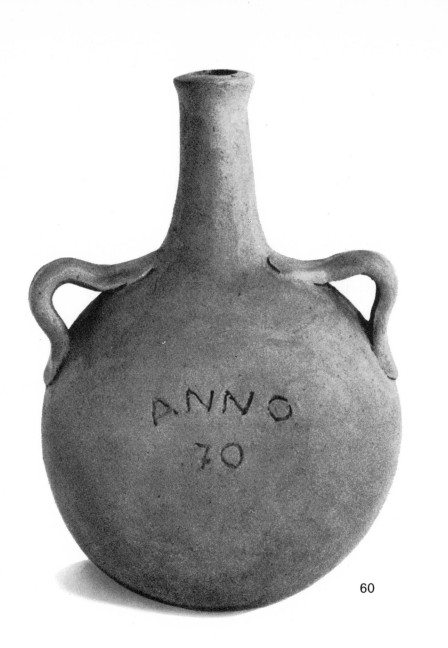

60

61

In the case of the little oil jar (61), the pouring rim and handle are added.
The clay bottle with lifting handles (60) was closed at the moulding opening (see 54) after we had smoothed the neck of the bottle from the inside.

62

63

In the contours of the base, belly, and shoulder of the vase (62) the hand may be recognised as the shaping instrument. The lines of the black dip engobe throw its plasticity into relief.
The drawn, evenly-tapered convex surface (63) has a base that was turned and pressed on the flat of the hand.

64

65

66

Pressure alters the surface of a hollow sphere that is still moist-hard.
By rolling, the convex cylindrical surface is formed between the sphere segments (64).
A sphere segment rolled around a chosen axis re-shapes itself to a cone (65). Lines of engobe, applied with a squirt-ball, emphasize and decorate the rolled walls (64, 65). The rolling technique is also the basis of the jar (66).

67

Round, flattened surfaces on a spherical body invite labelling (67). Inscriptions, etc., can be scratched in without difficulty on the dry engobed surfaces.

68

69

The ointment jar (68) is given a transparent glaze. Its origin in the sphere is clear. Wide moulding openings facilitate the flattening process, since counter-pressure may be applied from the inside.

Modification of the sphere by pressure offers a multitude of interesting variations. The cube (69) with wall surfaces pressed inwards also belongs in this category.

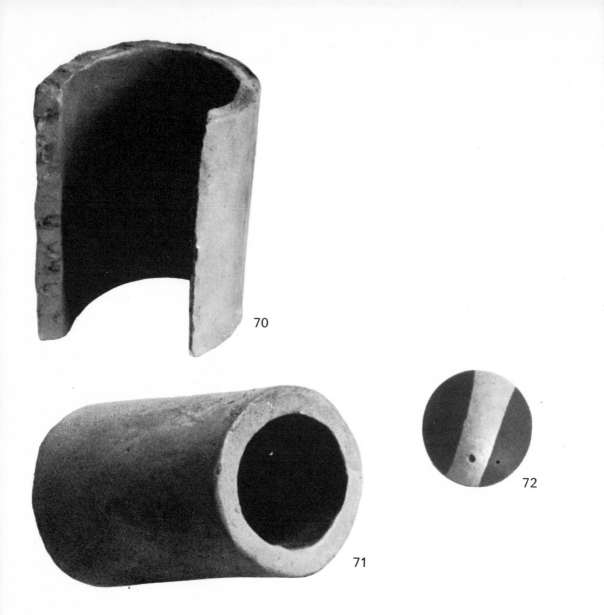

70

71

72

A flat mass of clay lies on a wooden board. With a rolling pin of 1–2 in. diameter we roll an even layer (like pastry). Repeated lifting and turning prevent the slab from sticking. It is cut with a knife and ruler according to the desired measurements.

58

73

74

Clay walls may be set up (70) and joined together. The clay tube (71) receives a flat base and an open moulded dome (73). Stripes of engobe, dipped and applied, subdivide the form (74).

75

76

Cylindrical body with a dipped and partially glazed surface (75). Small jar with the rim slightly drawn in, shiny inside and matt brown outside glaze (76).

The ball catcher (78), which has no base, can be inverted over the spotted hollow ball (77) or the one treated in areas (72).

77

78

79

80

The marking on the 'navel pot' (79) arrived by accident as the mass of clay was rolled out on a pastry board with a bore-hole in it. (Height of the original: $5\frac{3}{4}$ in.).

Air holes in the encircling band of the little stove (80) are punched out with a copper tube.

81

83

82

64

84

85

The slanting clay wall, cut as a conical segment, makes both firmly standing vessels (81 and 83) and a labile standing shape (82).

The little cup (84) and the mug with outward-curving and rounded-off rim to fit the mouth (85) strike a balance between the two standing shapes opposite.

86

87

A mass of clay, beaten into a cube (86), is divided into slabs with the wire cutter. When putting slabs together we must smooth the surface edges inside and outside. In this process clay is drawn from one wall to the other. The surfaces interlock (88). Clay box (89).

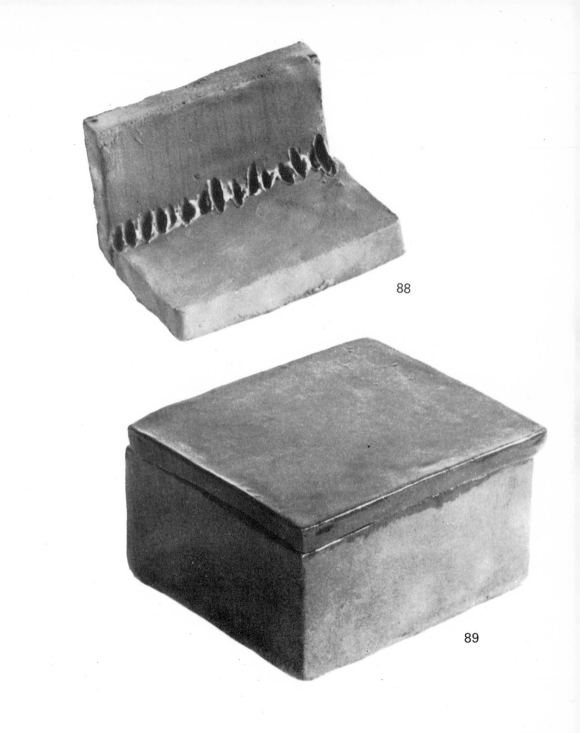

88

89

90

The walls of the container (90) are made by bending a flat strip. The pattern imprinted with a round-head screw suits the soft corners.

A clay block can be hollowed out with the wire scoop, smoothed with the finger, and made into a box-bowl (91).

Rectangular vase with engobe decoration (92).

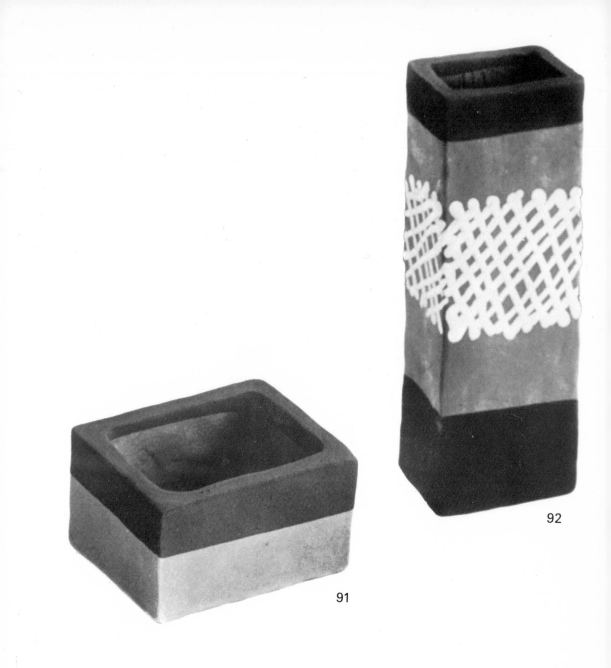

91

92

93

Sparkling glazes reflect a changing play of light from the walls of the vessels (93, 94).

94

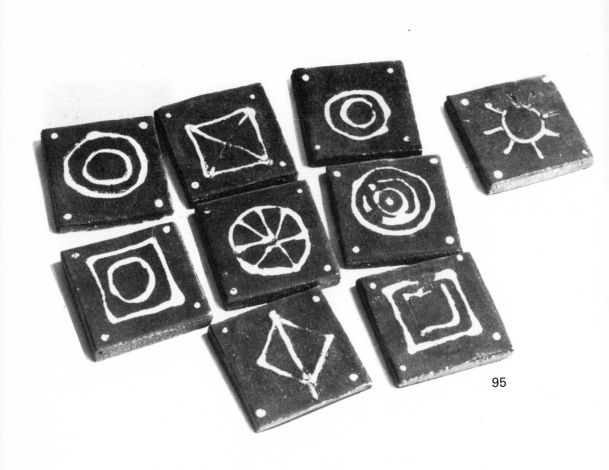

95

In drawing, pressing, and rolling, the clay works are kept to a manageable mass. If large containers are wanted, requiring more clay than can be properly handled as a mass, then a technique of building up is necessary.

For built-up ceramics, clays that have been thinned with grog, sand, etc., should be used. However, if we limit ourselves to vessels up to 12–16 in. high, we can try out the methods of building up with potter's clay.

In the building-up process pieces are placed one on the other. They may consist of flat pieces (95) or of pieces shaped however is desired. Thus the oil lamp is made of an arched base and upper portion (96).

In the coil method of building, rolls of clay are placed in an ascending spiral or in rings one above the other. These rolls are smoothed together after each layer, as the lower section will support the next layers only as it becomes firm. This method is not to be recommended for smaller vessels. Air bubbles and joins that have not been carefully smoothed together may produce tensions that will cause splitting.

Building with patches of clay makes it possible to create a great variety of shapes. Irregular patches, first kneaded with the hand, are joined together in the walls of the vessel to form a network and thus effect a durable union.

For built-up ceramics an edge cutter is suitable, if a turntable on ball-bearings can be turned evenly and easily. A piece of plastic should be placed under the clay base to avoid tiresome sticking. With hand-driven turntables one can even attempt the drawing up of little practice pieces. Thus we approach the potter's wheel.

96

97

98

On the voice amplifier (97) we see rolls that have not been completely smoothed together on the outside, kept as decoration. The vase (98) shows ribbon-like rings of flattened rolls.

99

The storage pot (99) is, like the pot (100) and the vase with a lid (101), made by the patch technique.

100

101

102

Clay pipe with cherry-wood stem (102).